Our Certain Way

The Building of a Legendary Pool Business

ALLAN CURTIS
SANDI MAKI

i

OUR CERTAIN WAY

ACKNOWLEDGEMENTS

As we began to focus on Our Certain Way of building pools we Started With Why and our new mantra really wrote itself:

Build the right projects, at the right pace, for the right customers, with a high level of quality, creativity and design. Enjoy the work.

This became our mantra, and as we found more and more special people to build for, this mantra helped us to create Our Certain Way.

To our Right Customers: we thank you for believing in us, and seeing the vision with us for your amazing back yards.

To our Team Members: we couldn't do this work without you. You each bring something special to our team, and we appreciate each one of you.

To our friends, and especially our mastermind group and marketing club members: you've been with us along this journey. Thank you for being our cheerleaders, celebrating our victories and helping us continue to grow.

Finally, to our contributing editor, Carol Pearson: you continue to help us grow and share our story with your commitment to finding the right words to help us shape our stories.

To our readers: you will find out in sharing our stories, we tell some from our individual perspectives. We also tell some from shared perspectives and don't always identify the speaker. We don't think it matters that much, so enjoy the read and get ready to guess whose story is whose! We hope you enjoy this journey in exploring Our Certain Way, and that it inspires you to think about yours.

Editors Note: Portions of this book first appeared in print in *AQUA Magazine* and are reprinted here by permission.

CONTENTS

EDITOR'S NOTES

Working on this project over the past several months has been a joy. Taking this truly deep dive into the Pool Guy's Certain Way, committing it to paper if you will, has helped it coalesce tangibly for me. Each time I send you a finished piece, I'm more and more excited by the results. And I'm having so much fun working on the book, and the parables. At the same time, I've been saying no to other projects that don't seem like a good fit, and finding more work that gives me joy.

My Certain Way. It's a beautiful thing. *You guys are the best.*

Carol Pearson, Contributing Editor

INTRODUCTION

I first met Al and Sandi in 2009 when they were guests being interviewed on a conference call with my network of business connections from around the country. They shared what they were doing with their company, building business and a brand through their use of social media, which was in its early days of being adopted by businesses.

From the start, they showed huge enthusiasm for transforming themselves through continual education, surrounding themselves with people who could influence them to be better, and through sharing their stories and experiences.

In these last years, I've watched with pride and excitement as they've continued to grow and share, while continuing to create the kind of exceptional lives that matter to them and to the world. Their business and personal lives stand as testament to the principles of my organization.

We are all blessed beyond measure, and the best way to express that blessing is to influence someone else's life for the better. This is Al and Sandi in a nutshell, and I'm proud to call them friends.

Dr. Tom Hill
Founder of the Tom Hill Institute and co-author
of *Chicken Soup for the Entrepreneurial Soul*

Al, Tom and Sandi at an Eagle Summit

FOREWORD

I've been in the pool business since the young age of 19, and the past quarter century has seen me up, down and sideways, all the time loving, and sometimes tolerating this unpredictable industry. The bitter cold spring days where we slog through mud, the relentlessly humid summers that sap all your strength, and the long cold winters where all I can think about is getting back out there again—it's a crazy life we all lead and have grown to love.

Through it all, I've truly found a way to speak my truth and create a business that makes me happy. Because happiness matters. It matters in business, and it matters in life.

That is why I felt compelled to write this book. Because it matters that much.

In this book, I'm talking to my colleagues in the pool industry—the commercial and residential pool builders and service people who are out there winter, spring, summer and fall, working to create and maintain those "happy places" for our customers.

I'm also writing to anyone who runs their own business or pursues their own passions, because I've found, happiness in what we do to make money truly does matter.

I hope you'll read this book and make an honest assessment of your own life, your own career or business. Finding your truth can be a challenge in this world full of ups, downs and opportunities. My truth is where my happiness lies, and I think you'll find yours there as well.

~Al Curtis

Part One–Business as Art, Work as Joy

"I don't build in order to have clients. I have clients in order to build."

~ *Howard Roarke*

1

WHY HAPPINESS MATTERS

"Forget about keeping your customers happy. Keep yourself happy in your work, and that joy can't help but infuse everything you touch."

~ Al Curtis

Slogging through some prep work at a new build one day in March, I had one of those crystal clear moments that change everything. It was pouring rain—the kind of icy cold rain that felt like frozen needles on this "spring" day in Michigan—I was aching and sore, standing up to my ankles in liquefied mud.

My body was screaming for mercy, having basically atrophied over the winter in this seasonal business I'm in, and I was soaked to the bone. The moment of clarity came when I realized—in spite of being wet, cold, hungry, sore and tired—I was whistling.

What I realized in that moment is that I was truly happy to be in this miserable pit of mud, because the vision in my head of what I was creating was far stronger than the physical discomfort I had to deal with in the moment.

That, my friends, is why happiness matters.

If you work for the money alone, you might be happy on one level because yes, you can enhance your life with the money and fund a lifestyle that makes you feel content. But can you really have true joy, true happiness if you don't flat out love the work? Could I have made it in to work the next day with a smile on my face if I didn't truly get joy out of what I do?

I doubt it.

To me, that is what happiness is all about: finding the love in the *thing* that you are doing, *because* you are doing it. Whether it hurts, whether it's painful or whether it's exhausting, it doesn't matter. What matters is finding the joy in this thing that allows it to be ok, no matter if I am tired, if I am sore or feeling lazy.

Forget About Happy Customers

The other day I was having a chat with a customer and another contractor on a job site. The contractor was saying "Oh, for us, it's really important that the customer is always happy."

In front of the customer, I stopped him and said, "I disagree."

I explained that I believe if I can find a way to

be happy in what I do, then the customer is guaranteed to be happy.

"But if I focus on the customer's happiness and try to do everything according to them, and I am not enjoying the process and I am not loving the process, then we all miss out because the customer won't be happy either," I continued.

Some customers, to be sure, won't agree to this approach. We learned the hard way a few years ago that we shouldn't be working for those people. Saying no is sometimes the most powerful way to find your own happiness and your own joy. For those who get it, the right projects are truly a joyful collaboration.

Steampunk Caribbean Legendary Escape

The Remarkable Energy of Happy

Interacting with customers and other contractors is great, and I cherish the relationships that I build. Still, for me there is a stronger sense of connection with water, with an experience, a true connection to creating an environment that people can experience happiness in.

Now, I grant you, if I just put in a pool, there will be some happiness created. Pools are a blast no matter who builds them. My goal goes beyond that, to create this sense of space that honors the land and honors the people who will use it. And that all has to do with water, which is what we're predominantly made up of. I truly believe in the law of attraction—like attracts like. Our bodies are made up primarily of water and are therefore attracted to water. If I can put the right energy into the water and do my very best to create a joyful space, then I am happy, the customers are happy—and I suspect that if we could look at the molecular level, that water is happy too!

Work Hard, Play Often

A key member of our crew is Penny, my adorable golden retriever. No matter what's going on, that silly dog makes me happy. You see, she serves as a constant reminder of the simple things in life and what's important—loyalty, friendship, and taking time to play.

Great example: I was digging a pool last month and she comes up to the excavator when I stop for a moment and she jumps up and drops her ball right in front of me. In other words, "Play with me. I don't care what you are doing, it doesn't matter what you are doing, and it's time to play."

I throw the ball, she runs and gets it, comes back and we do this several times and then she's good for a while. She constantly reminds me of the importance of letting go of what we think is so important, and showing me that there's always time for joy.

It's moments like these that I'm left wondering why me? Why do I lead such a blessed life to be able to surround myself with such awesomeness?

I believe it comes down to a couple of key things. First is an awareness of how awesome life is, and how grateful I am to share it with terrific people—customers, crews, partners, and folks like you in this industry. And secondly, and most importantly, letting that gratitude bubble up and fill me with joy.

"We are first artists—then creators of backyard water spaces."

~ Allan Curtis

2

HELLO GORGEOUS

I'm a true hybrid—a wild blend of pool guy, artist, philosopher, social media geek/guru, entrepreneur and family man—so building hybrid pools is a perfect fit for me. With every project I undertake, I push the limits of creativity, applying best practices in building techniques with new artistic expression. For me, hybrid pools offer unlimited opportunities to play and explore. And they've expanded my business in ways I've never dreamed possible.

I've been in the pool industry for almost my whole adult life, logging 28+ years in the business. Like you, I've seen new products, new trends and all sorts of innovations and I am always excited to learn something that I can pass on to my customers and help create the perfect backyard lifestyle.

My adventure into "hybrid" pools began years

ago when a customer wanted a traditional vinyl liner pool, but also wanted to put deck chairs in the shallow end and have a swim-up bar with stools that would sit in the water—possibly tearing the liner and causing expensive repairs.

I suggested a combination of two traditional pool building techniques; the body of the pool would be done with a traditional vinyl liner, and the sun shelf, swim-up bar and table areas would be crafted in gunite. The clients absolutely loved the idea, and my career in hybrid pools was launched. With hybrid pools, I can challenge the boundaries of what my customers expect, and deliver a truly life-enhancing addition to their home.

Some manufacturers are answering the demand for sun shelves and other such add-ons with fiberglass options that match the vinyl liners. That's one way to go, but I found my customers were still limited to what the manufacturer could supply, instead of a solution that will truly fit their lifestyle. I saw a tremendous opportunity in filling this unmet need.

"In matters of style, swim with the current; in matters of principle, stand like a rock."

~ *Thomas Jefferson*

Natural, Nautical Legendary Escape

Giving Them What They Want = Real Customer Satisfaction

As I begin the design process, I ask the homeowners how they see themselves using the space. How will the pool integrate into the rest of the yard, patio, walkways, and decking? Do they want a swim-up bar? Would they like deck furniture that sits on a sun shelf or shallow area of the pool? What about slides, grottos or other built-ins? (We did one hybrid project for a pizza-baking family that included a massive wood-fired brick oven integrated seamlessly into the overall design. It was a fantastic use of the hybrid pool's best features.)

The beauty in the hybrid is that we are only

limited by imagination and potential budget. Not only am I free to create new shapes, new designs and new functions for my customers, I can do it in ways that meet their needs exactly. By building hybrids, I automatically move myself out of the run-of-the-mill pool builder set and into the world of custom work. This is where I've built a lasting reputation as a creative and responsive pool builder who really understands my customers and what they want.

In this kind of space, online referrals seem to take care of themselves, and we've been able to take our pick of exciting and challenging projects. As more homeowners see these awesome hybrid pools, the general feeling seems to be "It's gorgeous, it's unexpected, it's art, and I want one!"

That is the best kind of feedback I can hope for.

"Do not hire a man who does your work for money, but him who does it for love of it."
~ *Henry David Thoreau*

"It's not just a pool.   It is an outdoor art gallery where you happen to get to swim."

~ Sandi Maki

3

WORK AS ART

We've all heard the old saying that if you love what you do, you'll never work another day in your life.

It rolls off the tongue like the cliché that it is. Life coaches preach the idea all the time, and motivational speakers tout the benefits of having a passion-driven career.

Yet a lot of people struggle with this idea. I know I used to. Like most of us, I was conditioned to view work as necessary, something to push through so we can enjoy the good stuff after hours, not something to truly enjoy in and of itself.

I believe this is because we are not conditioned to allow ourselves to be happy in the work we do. Instead, we think "*I have to do this so I can have these things.*" "*I have a mortgage payment so I have to make money.*" "*I have a family to raise...or car payments...or medical bills...or..."*

We all have this story in our heads that tells us we have to "work" in order to get to the good stuff. As a result of this story, we do the thing that we think will help us get that money.

Ask yourself honestly—why are you in the business you've chosen? Probably a large part, if not the main part, of your answer is because you expect to make money at it. You wouldn't do it if you didn't have some expectation of financial reward.

Now I know that money is very important. In our society, it's how things happen. However, I've come to realize that money is just a magnifier. If you're a happy person without money, having more money just magnifies that happiness. And if you're miserable without money, having more is just going to magnify your misery.

We only have to look at the tragic stories of huge lottery winners to see this in action. Seemingly unlimited wealth—something that many of us dream about—appears to cause more problems, heartaches and drama for so many of those "lucky" winners.

If money is only a magnifier, then why not choose happiness no matter where you are financially? Why not choose to do what you love? And if you can't do that, try loving what you do and find your passion in that.

Granted, not everyone is passionate about

everything they do in life. But you can be! It comes down to making a choice. I can choose to be happy in this particular situation, or I can choose not to be. I can choose to be excited and move forward, or choose to remain stuck right where I am.

Because make no mistake about it, happiness is a choice. In fact, a recent survey discovered that one of the most common regrets people have when they get to the end of their lives is not allowing themselves to be happier.[i] It seems we realize that this is our choice only when it's far too late to do anything about it.

So how does all this relate to your work?

For me, happiness and passion for what I am doing go hand in hand. If you're passionate about something, you're engaged in it, you are immersed and enjoying it. When you are enjoying it, you're happy! Many people find their passion in fishing, painting, writing, woodworking or other hobbies. And for some, they find their passion in the thing they do to make money.

That's what I've done with pools. I've consciously made the decision that I'm going to love what I do, and I'm only going to take on the work that I love. If it doesn't excite me, if I think it's going to be a drag, I turn down the job.

I learned from hard experience that if you keep taking miserable jobs that you don't want to do, it's a huge challenge to figure out how to find your passion there. I suppose you can convince yourself that you'll learn to like it, or at least like the results (i.e. the money), because it puts food on the table. But for me that is a recipe for misery.

Instead, you have to find those things that you do love about your business, that type of work that really does turn you on. And when you do that, lo and behold, your energy steps up because you like what you're doing. The right customers step up, because they feel your passion and your enthusiasm. The entire process builds and repeats itself, drawing more of the "right" kind of projects your way.

For me, that's how my work has become my art. I've learned to love the process and all the pieces of the project; there's no part of the work that I don't love. Even standing up to my knees in mud on a cold rainy day in March has a certain appeal when I can envision how I'll turn this giant pit of mud into a gorgeous backyard escape for my happy customers.

In doing this, the process and the work becomes part of me. When I work on something, that outcome is my legacy, it's a part of my personal legend, and I love it.

Now I happen to be on the construction side, but this idea applies equally to the service side, to renovation work, or to supplying the materials others need. Find the thing that you love about your current work, focus on that and you'll get plenty of work. Yes, at first you might have to take some jobs that aren't perfect. We all have to do this, especially when we are building our business. Nonetheless, **keep focused on that stuff you love**, and move closer to that with each job.

If you do this, if you can figure out what it is that you love to do and stay focused on the work you love, you'll get more of that work than you know what to do with.

Legendary Escapes Zen Waterfall

That's been the secret behind our growth at Legendary Escapes—we just decided to do what we love. That allows us to stay happy every day, and be passionate about the work. I can't wait to get to the job site to dig into the next step of the project. I'm always excited for what's next because it's so cool and so fun to design something new, and something we've never tried before.

That's me, every single day, doing work I love and turning it into my art. That's me, because I take on the work that I love. Work becomes play when I am truly passionate and engaged in what I do.

"The delicate balance of mentoring someone is not creating them in your own image, but giving them the opportunity to create themselves."

~ Steven Spielberg

4

THE LEARNING CURVE

As pool industry professionals, we are always learning, always expanding our skills. Whether your company installs a huge volume of manufactured pools or creates a handful of unique custom poolscapes, you learn something new with each job.

With the never-ending flow of new products and techniques, the learning curve is more like a spiral, a continually expanding cycle of learning that takes everyone in the industry up a notch with each turn.

Yet as professionals, we are often expected to be the "go-to" guys for our customers and others in the business. In that role, we must exude that confidence to be credible.

It can be a tricky balance—staying open to new ideas and new information, while at the same time being confident in our own skills so we can speak with authority.

As our "Ask the Pool Guy" brand has become more popular, my team and I often find ourselves in the position of being mentors to others in the industry. And I will tell you, it's a humbling experience to know that the words I say have meaning to someone else. It doesn't seem like that long ago that I was a rookie in this industry, soaking in all the knowledge I could and often learning the hard way.

Somewhere along the line I turned that corner and became a trusted source. Yet I'm always looking for ways to improve on my skills.

The same is true for my personal life. Everyone I meet has something in them that I can learn from and grow on.

I have opinions—really strong opinions—and these are most often based on personal experience. Physically seeing something and witnessing the results makes it real for me, makes it "true" if you will.

And that's what I try to project to others. I want you to trust in what I say not because I said it, but because it's based on some amount of hard evidence or proof.

You see, truth is a sliding scale: An event can happen, and four witnesses can report four entirely different experiences. We all see the world through our own set of filters, and this impacts the way our brains interpret things.

What's helped me continue to grow and

establish my authority is to recognize the mentors I've had in my life. Some of these mentors are well-known in the industry. Folks like David Tisherman, Brian Van Bower, Skip Phillips and Lew Akins have all inspired me—and probably many of you reading this book—by building amazing careers around their own unique style of projects.

These are the people I consider "industry mentors," and I am so grateful to what I've learned from them. Other people have influenced my life on a more personal level, helping to form the person I am and my underlying approach to work and to life.

Al with Jack Roberts, an early mentor

These kinds of mentors show up if you stay aware and open to learning. I truly believe that we can learn something from everyone we meet if we only allow ourselves to be open.

Continuing to grow in your craft requires a dedication to learning and evolving, and there are so many people you will meet along the way who can help. You never know who your next mentor is going to be and how they are going to change your life. All you have to do is slow down enough to see them.

"Creativity is just connecting things. When you ask creative people how they did something, they feel a little guilty because they didn't really do it, they just saw something. It seemed obvious to them after a while. That's because they were able to connect experiences they've had and synthesize new things."

~ *Steve Jobs*

5

THE SECRET LIVES OF STUFF

Reclaiming turns things into other things and that is like magic!

~ *Sandi Maki*

Our company is quickly earning a reputation for taking old things—stuff that many would consider junk—and repurposing them in a new way.

We do this not because we are part of the green movement, although there is certainly nothing wrong with that way of thinking. We don't do it to save money. On the contrary, it's often an expensive proposition to properly use reclaimed materials in our designs.

We do it for the simple reason that everything carries energy.

All the stuff in life, all the materials that go into the things we build, has its own energy. Everything carries a sense of where it came from and the history that it has witnessed. It is this history, this sense of past, that helps to create a rich and complex atmosphere in our projects.

Reclaimed Wine Bottle Lighting

Take barn wood for example. In my travels around Michigan, I often come across really old barns—100 or 200 years old—in danger of collapse. I enjoy talking to the owners and seeing if they'd be willing to part with the wood. I make it clear that I'm not going to burn it or destroy it, but instead lovingly and respectfully incorporate that material into a new project.

When we use this type of material, which by its very nature is a limited resource, we don't have the luxury of cutting it up any way we want and wasting any bit of. We can't just run to Home Depot and get more if we make a mistake.

Reclaiming Barn Wood

Using these old materials makes us more careful and more present with the project. As an artist, it forces me to think the project through in a caring manner, respecting the energy of the material and what it brings while limiting waste as much as possible.

Some people we've talked to ask how we can assure the quality of the reclaimed materials we use. Isn't it "safer" from a quality perspective to buy brand new materials?

If you think about quality from a strictly scientific perspective, maybe...but then again, just because something is new doesn't mean it is well made. Look at how quickly those expensive phones in our pockets break down and become garbage.

Quality, to me, comes from the emotional

connection we have to the materials we use. It's an esoteric kind of quality, not measurable with scientific instruments, but with the heart.

The weathered and worn feel of reclaimed material has a richness and warmth that can't be replicated with new materials. I believe this kind of craftsmanship can truly enrich our customers' lives.

The idealist in me likes the idea of taking something that's outlived its useful life and giving it a new purpose—like the old ship's lantern that was taking up space on a collector's shelf. By wiring it with low voltage lighting and building it into the project, we were able to return it to its original purpose of lighting a particular space with a modern treatment that makes it practical and highly functional.

About Character

Our aim is to create a backyard environment that has "character." I remember when I was a kid the family room was for family and daily living, while the living room was for guests only, with its plastic covered furniture that screamed "don't get too close."

We don't create our pools for company; we create them for hanging out, for the family. We like our pool environments to say "come and play with me, come enjoy me."

Reclaimed Lighting and Rope Accents

Certainly there are some stunning high end pools that are absolutely beautiful to look at but don't do much to invite us in to play, linger and relax. Using reclaimed items helps us create that old style of comfort that draws our homeowners in and beckons them to experience the entire pool.

For example, we recently used an old ship porthole built into the back of the grotto that you can actually open and stick your hand through. It adds great natural light in the grotto, and makes an interactive experience that was unlike anything we'd done before.

Authentic Ship Port Hole on the Grotto

We design our pools to be an organic experience from the start, which gives us the flexibility to create room for just the right piece. In our latest project, we initially proposed a "theming" budget to our customers, but the homeowner didn't really understand what that meant and decided not to add it in. As the project began to take shape—especially the waterfall and grotto features—the homeowners were able to walk into the grotto and have a look.

They were immediately reminded of a favorite childhood movie, "The Goonies," and mentioned that to our team. This got the creativity flowing, and we began to look at the grotto as a hideout for shipwrecked pirates who used the timbers from their ship to support the walls of a cave so they could live there.

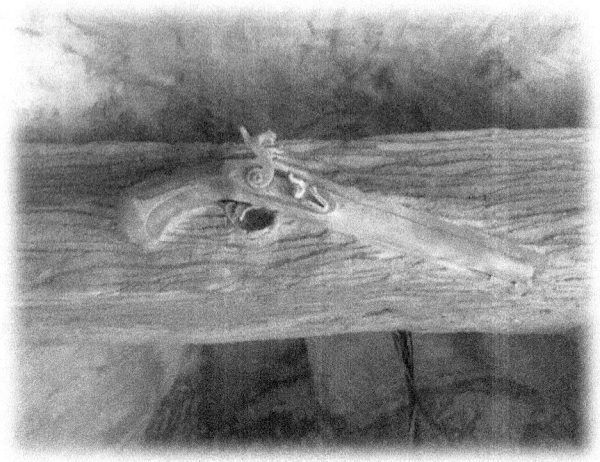

Carved Concrete Timber

Hand-carved cement "timbers," old rum barrels, even a custom crafted treasure chest complete with lighted "jewels" (tied in to the low-voltage lighting) will turn the grotto into a magical experience for *all* the kids in the family, young and old!

We completed our pirate adventure and the homeowner is so excited about their themed grotto, which they more clearly understand now that they can see how it is seamlessly incorporated into the overall design.

Hand Carved Barrel – By Karen

As an additional treat for the homeowner, our team was absent from the project for a couple days to travel to the international pool show, and we planted a pirate flag in our absence as one more fun surprise and point of conversation while we were away. It's this kind of magic—the relationship with our customers—that is the end result of all the creative energy we pour into our work.

"Truth is a point of view, but authenticity can't be faked."

~ *Peter Gruber*

6

THE POOL GUY'S JOURNEY TO A CERTAIN WAY

In all of our human pursuits, we develop ways of acting that have a dramatic effect on the outcome. How we treat our friends and family influences the kind of satisfaction we get from those relationships. How we treat strangers influences the kind of experiences we have and the energy we put out into the world.

It's the same with our work. How we approach the work we do has a huge impact on how fulfilled we feel at the end of the day, regardless of what that work may be.

When we work in a way that is true to ourselves, our "Certain Way" as I like to call it, we find not only success, but true happiness and satisfaction in what we create.

The challenge, for most of us, is figuring out just what our certain way is, and then committing to acting on it relentlessly in spite of whatever challenges come our way.

The Old Way (from Sandi's perspective)

It was twenty years ago when Al Curtis became owner of a swimming pool construction/service company. At the age of 26, Al already had seven years of experience in the business and was technically skilled at the work, but was woefully unequipped to handle the business end of things.

The vinyl pool business—purchased when the owner needed to retire for health reasons—was fairly healthy on paper through new pool sales, construction and service. But both the service and construction teams were poorly managed, and the monthly overhead was killer.

By sheer grit and determination, Al said "yes" to most anything, handling every lead and trying to turn every phone call into revenue. Customer service was disorganized, and the crews ran from job to job based on who was complaining the loudest.

It was no way to run a business, let alone create long term satisfaction. A few years in and Al had managed to put together some solid and friendly crews, and the business was doing okay. But there was something lacking; there was no "special something" that set Al's company apart from others in the market.

Still, he kept plugging, working the pool

business in the warm months, and any number of other revenue-making ideas in the offseason.

A Spark of Hope

After several years of this, Al was ready to let it go and try something new. Around this same time, I came in as a partner, through a series of coincidences that seem improbable in hindsight. We continued to work to grow the company for a few years, then decided to step away from the pool business for a while and create the InSights Group, a business networking community of like-minded people all focused on finding "a better way" to work, to live and to be happy.

Then something funny happened. Turning our attention away from the pool business allowed Al to set aside everything he knew and felt about it. And he found that he truly did love the work he was doing; he just needed to find a new way that would be more manageable, more profitable and, yes, more fun.

So we began asking ourselves: WHAT IF? What if we could build a company strictly doing the work we love to do? The other question we asked ourselves was WHY? Why do I want to do this, and why me? Why meant sharing our message, our passion for the industry and speaking out as an advocate. No one in the industry seemed to be working to raise the bar across the board, advocating for individual business owners, the inventors of cool new things, and giving a voice to the consumers. Al decided why not him...and "Ask the Pool Guy" was born.

Finding Authenticity and our Certain Way

Those critical questions: "What If?" and "Why?" began to shape everything about the business from that point on. It allowed us to clearly define what kind of projects we would take on, and what kind of people we wanted to work with. It helped us clarify the kind of people we wanted working on our crews, and in our office. We were able to say no to projects that weren't a good fit, and embrace the things we say yes to with our whole hearts.

Legendary Outdoor Adventure Pool

We became happy at work. Happy pool guys building happy pools for happy customers.

Along the way we created our cool signature Hybrid Swimming Pool concept and have found a level of creative freedom and joy we didn't know could exist in this business. We've made cherished friends out of customers along the way, and have been embraced as advocates by others in the industry. We have a huge social media following and a robust online presence. We also love the work we do and the people we do it with.

We've found our Certain Way. It all started with asking WHAT IF and WHY.

Part Two–Your Business, Your Way

"I take on the work that I love. Work becomes play when I am truly passionate and engaged in what I do."

~ Allan Curtis

7

SANDI'S WHY

"Imagine a world where people wake up every day inspired to go to work, feel safe while they are there, and return home at the end of the day feeling fulfilled by the work they do, feeling that they have contributed to something greater than themselves."

~ *Simon Sinek*

Let these words from Simon Sinek, author of the viral mega-hit book and motivational video *Start with Why*,[ii] sink in for a few moments.

Is this kind of world even within the realm of your imagination? Or are you, like so many others, cynical that we can find or create those kinds of workplaces and build those kinds of incredibly satisfying careers?

Is it possible to find fulfillment building pools?

For so many people, their work is simply something they must do, something that pays the bills. Sure, they may enjoy it. There may even be days when they could say they love it. Overall though, the weekend can't get here soon enough, right?

I used to feel this way about my work and the various jobs I held, until I discovered my own why.

I'm often asked—by customers, suppliers and other people in the industry—how I ended up as The Pool Girl, co-owner of Legendary Escapes with Al Curtis. Of all the possible careers open to me, why am I here?

It all started about a dozen years ago when I had the opportunity to join the pool company, as I wrote about in the last chapter. At the time I was a single mom with two kids to support. The pool company offered a decent paycheck, flexibility when I needed it for the kids, and an opportunity to help grow a business from the inside out.

Saying yes was easy. The larger question is: Why have I stayed when I've had so many other choices over the years?

With a four-year college degree in Psychology and a solid background in marketing, there were any number of other ways I could spend my time that were a lot more glamorous than standing butt deep in pool water or ankle deep in mud.

Sandi's Kids on the Job

While these opportunities paraded before me, there were times I was tempted. I stayed because the pool industry in general, and this company in particular, ultimately began to be the place where I could find the kind of fulfillment that only comes from living my own why.

I remember as a kid one of my all-time favorite books was *The Handy Girls Can Fix It* (Peggy Kahn, 1984).[iii]

The book was about a group of girls who liked to work with their hands and began to offer their services doing painting, gardening and other odd jobs around the neighborhood. Eventually they help two younger kids in the neighborhood by creating a clubhouse for them, and discover how much fun it is to give back.

What has always stayed with me is the cool vibe of the clubhouse atmosphere; as I read that book again and again I could feel how awesome it must have been to be in that group, with everyone contributing their particular talents to make the experience the best it can be.

It makes perfect sense then that I fell in love with the pool business. Our company has always offered an encouraging, supportive environment, in which each person can contribute their own personal talents to the whole. Now that I am co-captain of this ship, I focus on this legacy and work hard to maintain and grow that atmosphere, from the front office to the field.

In the course of creating this company, we've also create a clubhouse for grownups. Al and I love surrounding ourselves with interesting things and interesting people, so it seemed like a natural extension of our work to open a clubhouse where business owners could share and contribute and enjoy hanging out.

Our "office" space has expanded over the years to include meeting rooms and lounge areas where our club members and friends can drop in, hang out, learn from each other and find support.

An Office Mural and Low Voltage Lighting

Through our Mastermind and marketing groups, we help small business owners discover their own why, and help them learn how to market their business using organic marketing principles that truly work for them, the same principles we'll introduce at the end of this book.

Through our work with young people in the community, we see them discover their talents and grow as individuals, while they realize that we are all life-long learners regardless of our educational backgrounds or pursuits.

Through our work with our own pool crews and office staff, we take this same kind of supportive approach. Our team also happens to be predominantly women, both in the office and on the construction team. This is not because we set out to hire more women than men, it's because so many young women started to ask if they could work with us, and as it turns out they enjoy the work and do an outstanding job when they do. We are able to accomplish great things, with our very non-typical construction crew.

Our entire team is included in discussions of our collective "Why". We also go over each individual's "Why" at our weekly team meetings, including the important question of their role on our team: "Does it make you happy?" The end goal for our workers is not to stay in the pool industry forever—unless that's what they truly want to do, and in that case we'll support them in any way we can. Rather it's to empower them to find their own why, and find the courage to go seek that out in a big, bold way.

As I reflect again on Simon's words, I can imagine that kind of world, that kind of career. I've helped to create it, and I consider it a rare and beautiful privilege to go to work with these people every day.

I hope you'll take a moment to reflect on your inner Why, and bring more of that into the world.

What can you imagine? What is your Why?

"We do not stop playing because we grow old. We grow old because we stop playing."
~ Benjamin Franklin

8

SELLING YOU

"Be genuine.
Be remarkable.
Be worth connecting with."

~ Seth Godin

Marketing Guru Seth Godin refers to it as the connection economy—a new reality that is forcing business owners to make the switch from being "order takers" to trusted authorities.

As Godin said in a recent blog post, "the traveling salesman, the carnival barker and the old-time businessman can hit and run. Make the sale, cut your costs, move on."

In that old-school "transactional selling" model, there's no relationship past the immediate purchase. Maybe they remember you and call you back next season, or maybe they call the guys down the road. It makes no difference to them; your business is just one of many and the bottom line is generally price or availability. While transactional selling may be working for your company now, it doesn't leave the door open for long-term growth in an industry like ours. Instead of growing your business, you spend a hefty chunk of your time and efforts regaining customers you already thought you had, and struggling to stand out in a big pool of competitors.

Al and Seth Godin in NYC

What would it mean to your business if customers sought you out, instead of the other way around? What if people called you because they heard about you from a friend or saw your post on Facebook, or remembered meeting you from a how-to video they viewed online?

In my own experience as owner of Legendary Escapes, it changes everything.

We used to spend a lot of time on our outbound marketing; sending postcards, flyers, advertising. We started building an online presence around 2007, connecting with customers, friends and prospects and building great relationships with folks online. We based it on a friendly "Pool Guy" character, and started publishing content with the theme of "Ask the Pool Guy."

We focused on creating useful and fun content, like how-to videos, informative blog posts, photos of our favorite projects—all aimed at helping pool owners get more out of their backyards. By establishing a fun and professional presence in our blog, Facebook page and video channel, we started to make the switch from transactional selling to relationship selling.

This kind of outreach makes all the difference in our sales process. Research proves that social media (Facebook, Pinterest, Twitter and the up and coming social sites) are the fastest growing consumer sources for influencing purchase decisions. Having a solid presence online gives us a huge boost.

By the time the customer calls us, they feel like they know me already from my online presence, they know my work and how I go about the job. So the hard part of the sale—building trust—is already done by the time I sit down with them face to face.

The giant bald-headed caricature of me as The Pool Guy splashed across the side of the company vans doesn't hurt either. And it's a blast when I meet a new customer and they give me a big handshake, a slap on the back and say "Hey, Pool Guy!" like they've known me for years.

In any field, you've got to find a way to make yourself stand out. You can have the best service, the best products, the best prices, but if nobody can tell you apart from the other guys, what's the point?

If you aren't building an authoritative presence online, where customers and prospects can find you, connect with you and begin to build a relationship with you, you are stuck in a transactional economy where price becomes the determining factor and brand loyalty is nonexistent.

"In a busy marketplace, not standing out is the same as being invisible."

~ Seth Godin

9

DIME A DOZEN: DEFINING YOUR NICHE

I remember the moment like it was yesterday. I was just leaving Home Depot with a random sack of fittings for a job, when I spotted a man hanging around my company van.

My first thought was "oh great, what is this guy up to," not sure what he was after standing next to my well worn construction van. As I picked up my pace, puffed out my chest and donned my best "ready for anything" face, the man saw me coming, broke into a big grin and said "Hey, Pool Guy, I've got a question to ask ya!"

That's when I knew there would be no trouble; I was being sought out for my industry expertise. What a great realization, and a fun confirmation that our niche marketing concept was truly working.

Al and the Truck {for AQUA Magazine}

In this mammoth $51 billion dollar a year industry[iv], defining your own niche can be a real challenge.

The first step is to decide what you want your niche to be, what you hope to accomplish with your marketing. For us, we had two major goals: 1) to set Legendary Escapes apart as a boutique custom pool company; and 2) to create a human voice and a solid presence in our industry and a position as experts in pool construction and service.

We had noticed that there wasn't any one person speaking as a resource for the industry— for pool builders, manufacturers, and homeowners. There was a real lack of a "go to" guy for these kinds of questions.

Our CMO Sandi Maki was the brains behind the actual marketing plan to build our niche. We started to build a persona—"Ask the Pool Guy"— who was a source of information for manufacturers, suppliers, other pool builders and customers. We began posting informational videos on YouTube, blogging weekly, and engaging in social media in all kinds of pool and outdoor lifestyle discussions.

We started going to local and national pool conventions, filming videos and doing on-the-spot Q & A sessions, and talking to everyone we could meet in the industry. We had "Ask the Pool Guy" images plastered over everything—and I do mean everything: trucks, vans, pens, t-shirts, puzzles, coffee mugs, towels, blankets, boxer shorts, the crew's work gear, M & M's Candies, and of course all over social media.

I didn't have an end game at these events. I just went to talk to people, share our ideas, give them a chance to talk about their business and share our passion for ours.

Before we knew it, the "Ask the Pool Guy" persona became a real presence both online and in real time, with people recognizing me and the crew as if they knew us. Because really, with our heavy social media and live network presence, they did, in many ways, know us already.

With this new found "celebrity" we were able to build Legendary Escapes into the boutique business we knew it should be—manned by a small crew of dedicated and talented people who are passionate about what we create and deliver. The more we engaged, the more our reputation grew and we are now in the fantastic position of being able to pick and choose the projects we take on each year.

Trade Show Video Work

We have the outrageous fortune to be able to work with people who understand our passion and feel the same. If our heart-felt approach to the craft doesn't make sense to someone, they're probably not our kind of customer. And that's okay! There are other pool companies that can meet their needs.

If I had to give you just one piece of advice, it's this: Just keep showing up. At industry events, at local networking events, on social media—show up to learn, to connect, to grow your knowledge base and increase your influence. Don't look for a specific return on investment for this time. It's not about how much you sell at a particular event, or how many business cards you collect. It's about all the folks you meet, the knowledge you offer, and engaging with the influential people in your industry.

It's in these things that your niche comes to life.

"The building blocks of the universe are water, concrete and vinyl."

~ Al Curtis

10

MAKING THE LEAP

So many of us start out in this business building pools for the mass market; basic designs for basic budgets, nothing really special or unique, but there's plenty of customers to buy what we are building. If volume is your thing, then this might be a business model that makes good sense.

Hybrid Swimming Pool, Legendary Escapes

For us, this wasn't the kind of business we wanted. Rather than quantity, we were hungry for creativity. We didn't care so much about how many pools we built; we just wanted each of them to be truly unique. And we wanted to do it locally, staying in southeast Michigan while we grew.

Crazy? Maybe, but it's not the first time I've been accused of that (and probably not the last).

Granted, Michigan is not the first place you think of as a hot spot for the pool industry. Between the tough climate (we have just a few good months of pool weather every year) and the economy (Michigan is always among the first to feel the pinch, and the last to recover) we've got our share of challenges.

We did it anyway.

In thinking back on how we did it, how we built a high-end artistic hybrid pool company by tapping our local market, I realized there were three major turning points for us along the way.

Famous for What?

I spent a lot of time researching and paying attention to builders that were known for original, creative projects instead of building standard, basic-budget pools. I studied the types of projects they built, the materials they were using, and the ways they were putting their projects together. I became really good at identifying each local builder by their individual style. From this knowledge I envisioned the kinds of pools I would build when I had the budgets they were working with. In other words, I started to define what I'd be known for—completely custom artistic hybrid pools.

I realized, as I studied the companies that I admired that were doing this, that they were dealing with an entirely different type of clientele.

They certainly weren't the kind of client I was used to having, with set budgets and set expectations as to what a "pool" means. So I asked myself, "How can I find a client who is willing to hire me to do this different thing I want to try?"

As I talked to more and more prospects, I found a very receptive audience when I suggest a new idea or an unusual design. The key was in having a clear idea of the kinds of pools I wanted to build, and asking my clients to let me do it. Once I could articulate my vision, they began to say yes.

How Much are You Worth?

I've shared this story before, about my customer who was so pleased with the final results that he told me flat out I could have charged 50% more for the project and he would have happily cut me a check. This blew me away, as I began to realize that not only were my skills and craft advancing with each project, my value was going up accordingly.

People were not just buying my pool building

skills; they were not buying the concrete and the boulders and the rock and the tile. They were buying my art and my creativity, the part of my business that feeds my soul and keeps me slogging through the concrete day after day.

Sure, there were some new things we tried that we didn't make a ton of money on. But we never gave our work away, like some folks in the industry recommend. Once you realize what you are worth, you can charge accordingly without hesitation. This is a critical step in finding clients with those dream budgets. They don't expect you to work for cheap; they expect to pay for the skills you bring to the project.

We started out building $25K pools, then made the leap to $30-40K pools. At the time, that seemed like a huge, scary leap to make. But we did it, and we pushed on. The leap to $50K was a turning point for us, so much so that the next big jump, to $75K, didn't feel like such a big jump after all. From there, we thought if we can build a $75K pool, why not $100K or $150K, and so on. It's just a number on a piece of paper, after all.

Tell the Right Story

What we quickly realized is our ideal customer is not looking for a pool, they are hoping to create a lifestyle experience in their backyard. To provide that, we have to know why they are spending that kind of money, and understand what they expect to get out of it.

They weren't doing it to impress their neighbors, or improve their property value. They were doing it to create an experience that suited their family, something specifically and uniquely their own.

Once we knew this, we could market to this audience using messaging that would resonate. We knew we were only going to get a very small percentage of the local pool buying market—and we were totally okay with that. We now had a voice and story to share that would resonate with the right clients, the ones who were looking for what we had to offer.

Social media and online marketing was the perfect vehicle for our marketing, as we were able to tap into an audience that was really receptive to what we had to say.

Ultimately, it was this process—defining what we wanted to do; understanding the value of what we offer; and telling the right story to the right people—that got us out of that basic "starter pool" mentality and helped us create a thriving niche business that we love.

"Saying 'yes' to one thing means saying 'no' to another. That's why decisions can be hard sometimes."

~ *Sean Covey*

11

HOW "NO" CAN HELP BUILD YOUR DREAMS

The customer is always right.
Except when they are wrong.

Traditional business models tell us that to succeed in our chosen field we need to cater to the customers and do what they like. To a point, this is true. You won't have much success as a bartender if you refuse to mix drinks for your customers.

Yet in the new connection economy, *who* you choose to do business with is as important as *what* you choose to do.

Not everyone *should* be your customer, and learning to turn down potential business can be terrifying and seem counter-intuitive. Yet creating a business that truly feeds your soul depends on doing just that, and it starts with knowing your true value in the marketplace.

For me, the paradigm shift began at the end of a particularly challenging project. The homeowner was beyond thrilled with the results. As he happily wrote me the final check, he turned to me and said, "You know, you could have charged me 50% more for this project and I would have paid it, no question."

I was stunned.

On the drive home I thought about what he said, and realized I had been undervaluing my work, charging what I thought the average pool owner would want to pay. Clearly I was worth much more than I thought; having this pointed out to me by one of my own customers was a light bulb moment.

People were not just buying my pool building skills; they're not buying the concrete and the boulders and the rock and the tile. They were buying my art and my creativity, the part of my business that feeds my soul and keeps me slogging through the concrete day after day.

And then it hit me. I didn't want to work for the average pool owner. My work, and especially my prices, would not appeal to them, and that's totally okay. I could shift away from the material part of what they were buying, to the esoteric.

My ideal customer, I realized, would be the property owner who wants something out of the ordinary, something epic even, and is willing to give me the artistic leeway to create that vision.

That's not to say that the client doesn't have a say in the final outcome; that would be ridiculous. We agree on rough plans and sketches, models and renderings. The leeway I'm talking about is a freedom to modify the plans as inspiration strikes, to choose the right color for the tile without the customer having to obsess over every detail, the ability to add on when the muses strike.

Art in the Grotto, Carved by Karen

With this shift came the understanding that we had to move from the "I'll take on any project" to being highly selective in who we work with. This did not come easy; turning down someone who is waving the money around can seem like a crazy move.

Saying no is a choice, and it's a decision we don't take lightly.

How do we decide who gets the "yes"? Sometimes you just know, so it can be hard to define. Still, if I had to break it down, it comes down to three characteristics:

~ Being the right customer
~ With the right attitude
~ And the right energy

The "right" customer is someone who has at least a six-figure budget for the entire project and is not afraid to spend it. They must have a suitable property on which the project will live, and be looking for something that will add lasting value to that property.

The right attitude means that they recognize the artistry and spontaneity that goes into one of our projects and they respect the creative process. They have a basic idea of the kind of environment they want, and are looking to us to materialize that idea, far beyond anything they could have imagined.

Finally, the right energy is key—positive, free flowing, trusting in us and confident in our abilities. The right customer is not hung up on the minutiae of the day-to-day build but relaxed and accepting that, like any work of art, plans change, things evolve, stuff happens and they are willing to flow with that.

When we meet potential customers with this combination, magic happens from the start and we quickly know whether or not we want to work with them, and they with us, which is really just as important.

Al and the Sanders -The Right Customers

If the magic isn't there, if something just feels off, we politely but firmly decline. The wrong customers have tried to cajole us, bully us, even threaten us to provide a quote, but if we don't feel the situation will be successful, why waste everyone's time?

It's taken us many years to get to this point, partly because you must hone your craft and know what you're doing before you can afford to take this approach.

If I knew now what I didn't know back then, I would have said "no" much more often. For us, it has been the key to the undreamt-of success we have been experiencing the past few years.

"You can do anything, but not everything."
~ David Allen

12

THE BOUTIQUE EFFECT

In business school, we often learn that the way to make more money is to grow. We take courses on how to grow, how to scale, how to get bigger, how to manage the growth—making the assumption that bigger means more profit at the end of the day.

But it's not necessarily the only way to make more money, especially in a business like ours. From my experience in this industry, I see two basic ways that companies can make more money: They can scale up, or they can add value with the boutique model.

Scaling Up and the Opportunity Cost

In the pool business, we all know the stories of the companies that have chosen to scale up. Many of them have done a fantastic job of it.

They find a type of pool they can build for a big client base, and they focus on selling more and more of them. It can work, but it's not without a cost.

The difficulty with this model lies in the things that go along with the scaling up. More work means more trucks, more crews, more office space and overhead. It means higher personnel costs and layers of staff and management to handle everything, and more customer service.

Of course, successful businesses have dealt with these challenges for years. Most guys and gals in this industry build companies by sitting behind desks and managing sales people, and the company grows that way.

What a volume-based company can't do very well is innovate. Because it relies on systems and procedures to produce that high volume, creativity and artistry is often relegated to new color choices in tiles or ready-made add-ons. Keeping the choices down also keeps the end costs in line, a highly important aspect of a volume-based business.

Adding Value and the Creative Process

What we've discovered is another way to make more money. Rather than scale in size, you can scale in value, following the boutique model, offering something really special that no one else in our area was doing.

Instead of getting bigger, we chose to get

better at what we do. With each project we focus on creating new solutions and innovating our design and execution. We don't do more work than we used to, but we do it whole a lot better.

The end result is that we produce a tiny supply (only a handful of pool projects in any given season) to the absolute best of our ability, pouring our passion and our creativity into each one. This combination of limited supply and higher value creates a huge demand and justifies a premium price. It's the law of supply and demand in action, and it has allowed us to make more money without doing more "work."

The Boutique Effect

Consider the concept of the boutique experience. The trendiest—and priciest—big-city hotels offer a limited number of rooms, which have to be reserved months in advance. The swankiest restaurants offer small dining rooms and a minuscule chance of scoring a table on date night. These establishments can and do charge a premium—and their customers gladly pay it because they understand the value of what they are paying for.

All too often a successful restaurant is convinced to open a second, third, fourth location, or even sell franchise locations. And almost invariably, the new locations just aren't as good as the original. Why? Because the original team that made it so terrific can't be in two, three or four places at once. The magic is somehow lost when it's spread out. Truly valuable work takes creativity and careful attention to each detail, something this is all too often lost when the work scales up.

The franchise model works great for products and services that don't require ongoing creativity and innovation in execution and delivery. It does require rigorous training of staff (think Starbucks baristas) and an easy-to-replicate experience for each customer.

And if that's the model you want to work with, that's great; many business empires have been made that way. But understand that you'll have a lot more competition at that level of business—you'll be forced to compete on price, service, time and other factors that can eat away at your profits.

The Authenticity Mandate

The challenge in accepting a boutique pool model requires us to stay authentically true to ourselves and the work we do. We are often asked to take on projects that don't fit our ideal job. And it has taken a lot of determination to learn when to say no. If you are just saying yes to every job that comes your way, you never focus on your sweet spot, a fact that took me years to truly understand.

Creating Art in a Legendary Escape

That sweet spot for us means less, not more, projects. Our brand is getting much bigger every year, thanks to our marketing and some fantastic word of mouth. We often have people come up to us and beg us to take on their project, asking if we please can just fit them in somewhere. And this is certainly not because of any lack of pool building companies in our area!

We've found that as we limit the work we take on, each project has more meaning to us and more perceived value in the world. We have the potential for exponential growth not by doing more, but by limiting the supply and create a true demand for it.

Part Three–About the Industry

"The trend toward customer-driven change means there is money in this industry for those willing to walk on the leading edge."
~ *Al Curtis, "Ask the Pool Guy"*

13

RAISING THE BAR

We get a lot of questions from pool owners—and from other pool companies—looking for more information on how we create our hybrid vinyl/gunite pools. For us, the process is a synergy; it's pieces from different types of projects, different types of pools, pulled together in new ways to create the optimal backyard environment.

The hybrid pools we create are in response to a growing trend: Customers are becoming more discerning and more specific all the time about what they want. It's no longer "keeping up with Joneses" and building what their neighbor has only bigger. Instead, we hear customers tell us how they want to use their outdoor space, what they want their lifestyle to be like, and it's these wishes that influence the design.

In building these more complex environments, it's not necessarily about discovering a brand new product or technique. Rather, it's about taking what's already known to work and readily available, and appropriating it in a new way.

What I love about our work is the creativity of it all. Instead of saying "well, we've always done it this way" or having our customers pick a design out of a book and plunking in the pieces, we like to say "what if" What if we use the same products we are familiar with, but we use some of this over here, and blend in a little of that over there.

And that's what a hybrid pool is all about. It's taking all the benefits of vinyl—the comfort, the ease of use, the durability, the way it handles the water chemistry and stands up to the weather—and combining that with the durability and flexibility of custom gunite elements—a sun shelf that will hold barstools, that hidden grotto or spill-over spa, and all those elements that require a different treatment than vinyl.

Where Vinyl Meets Gunite

We've arrived at this hybrid place because we kept trying different ways of working with the existing products, and we realized that when we used everything that was available in a new way, magic happens. I mean real "wow, I had no idea our pool could look like this" kind of magic.

This kind of creative innovation is being driven by our customers, and their desire for something unique that truly expresses the kind of leisure life they are looking for. And this kind of change—driven by customer demand—means there is money in this industry for those of us willing to walk on the leading edge.

This leading edge is where I believe our industry needs to change. Pool design innovation has always been driven from the gunite side, because it's fabricated on site. Vinyl and fiberglass pools are more product-driven, i.e. you pick your shape out of the product catalog, and we'll build that for you. Yes, we can do some design around that with some gunite features, but the basic shape is limited by the product.

That could change, and I believe the time is right for some of the leading vinyl designers to embrace this idea.

What I would love to see is designers in the vinyl liner industry come to the forefront. The well-known designers in our industry—the guys who have created incredible things and taken pools to the next level—are all gunite guys. Now there are some well-known vinyl names, sure, known for both the quality and quantity of their products, but we don't read much about these vinyl designers working on the front edge of custom pool design.

This is the road not traveled much at all...not reinventing the idea of a vinyl liner pool, but reimagining how it all goes together and offering vinyl liners that are custom-designed.

This idea, where we can use the existing benefits of vinyl in a bespoke way, is where we can blow the customers away.

If we look back to how the pool industry got where it is today, concrete pools were the original pools, then vinyl and fiberglass, but so many consumers still think that the only truly customizable options are in concrete. And our industry perpetuates that belief by keeping our design consultations product-focused. And to me that is the wrong approach.

Instead, we need to ask the deeper questions up front about what they expect out of their pool environment, and then design an environment to meet that request. There is a tremendous amount of design work that can be done in vinyl. We work with some terrific vinyl providers who provide the customization that we need, using standard panels that are put together in non-standard ways, repurposing instead of reinventing.

Right now I believe there is a huge opportunity for these designers to step up and showcase what they can do instead of offering the "pick one" approach.

The hybrid pool is more than a trend; this is happening as a result of customer demand and a changing market. The vinyl industry leaders are not necessarily addressing it fully...but they will. They'll follow the money, like all industries.

Instead of following the money, why not try leading the pack? What if we ask ourselves what more could we do for our customers? Be an early adapter, living on the front edge of that bell curve where all the innovation happens, not the long tail. Yes, you're taking risks—but isn't staying where you are and being a follower also a risk?

The customer is driving change in all industries, insisting on more custom solutions and less "out of the box" thinking. We will either be pushed in that direction, or we can innovate and bring it to the customer. This is where the opportunity lives, in any industry.

Sure it requires more time up front on the design end, but the finished product—and the customer relationship—will be a hundred times better for it.

"Quality is not an act, it is a habit."

~ Aristotle

14

THE ART AND SCIENCE OF QUALITY

Quality—we all want it, chase after it, and often pay more for it. Yet how much do we really understand quality and how to achieve it?

For people who work in the field of quality assurance, quality is measurable, definable to strict standards and metrics. Still, so much of what gives a product or service its true value is immeasurable, at least by any scientific standards.

Even the dictionary definition allows a huge degree of subjectivity on the topic: "The standard of something as measured against other things of a similar kind; the degree of excellence of something; a high level of value or excellence" is how Merriam-Webster defines the term, leaving it wide open for not just interpretation, but comparison.

So how do we define quality when it comes to our own businesses?

Quality can happen in many forms. In the pool business, we can use superior materials, put together in the standard way, to achieve quality. Or we can use regular grade products and put them together in a way for a new result that exceeds the original. We can even use subpar materials—reclaimed wood, broken glass, rusty metal—and put them together in the most spectacular way so that it answers a completely different definition of "quality."

You see, on the physical level, quality happens when you use science. The best mix of aggregates in your concrete, combined with exactly the right amount of water at precise temperatures, cured and poured perfectly make for a scientifically-proven level of quality.

But for most of us, quality happens on an emotional level. If something is of superior value, it just feels better, smoother, more solid, more lasting. It feels luxurious or one-of-a-kind in a way that makes us love it and want to have it in our lives.

For me, as a pool builder, I come at quality from an energetic standpoint. Far beyond just choosing quality materials, I direct my team to use those materials in the spirit of excellence, doing our best with what we have and giving our all to the job.

I have a customer who used to sneak out at night after the crew went home and check the day's progress with his levels and tape measures.

That's okay; he has a scientific mind and that was his way of reassuring himself that we were doing good work.

His wife, on the other hand, is more of an artistic soul and would catch herself watching the crew from her office window while they worked. She told me she could see that each of us were leaving a little something of ourselves at the job site each day, in the way we relished the work we did and threw our passion and our spirits into it.

For both the scientist and the artist, they saw quality in our process, and that leads to excellence in the final product.

It means attention to all the little details, the color combinations, the textures and how they all work together. Quality makes us feel better. There's love in it, passion in it, and an excitement for what we're doing. We've become masters of combining the pieces together to create an environment that speaks of high quality.

Look at Picasso and his artwork. Does his quality spring from the finest paper or canvas, the best inks or paints? No, it was the passion and talent he put into it that allowed him to create beauty that has endured.

We take that artistic approach in the hybrid pools we create, taking the standard materials available to anyone in the industry and adapting them for our needs. For example, we use a prefab tiling system from TRU-tile by Latham Industries. They make a great product that works really well with our hybrid design. But there was always one trouble spot...the skimmer face plate.

Vinyl Skimmer Modified in Tru-Tile Track

The way the system is designed, the finished plate sticks out almost an inch from the tile. Functionally, that's fine, but we feel it detracts from the finished product. So we've created a technique where we inset the face plate so it's flush with the tile. A somewhat minor detail, to be sure, yet it's the hundreds and thousands of those minor details that define our overall quality.

We've created a culture of quality that's part science, part art and all heart. I tell my crew members that if they don't love what they are doing—every shovel full of dirt and barrow full of concrete—they should look for other work, because the energy of what we're doing is just as important as the quality of the materials. When everyone loves what they do, there's love in the mix. And that, my friends, is at the heart of a quality business.

Karen and a barrow full of concrete

"Be a yardstick of quality. Some people aren't used to an environment where excellence is expected."

~ *Steve Jobs*

15

ON THE VALUE OF TRADE SHOWS

In the early days of my pool career, I worked for a builder here in Michigan. From the start I constantly wanted to learn more. I pored over the magazines that came through the office, devoured the few books I could find on the subject, and constantly bugged my boss about going to the trade shows.

He was more interested in keeping the status quo than in expanding his horizons, and the pool shows were just not on his radar screen.

It's not that he didn't learn about new products; he would talk to the sales reps that came by with the latest pump or new gadget, and if it looked like something that could make his life easier without having to adapt the way he did things, he would use it.

Meanwhile, I was always curious and wanting to be ahead of the curve, always imagining new solutions to the challenges we faced in the field every day.

Several years later, after buying the company, we were struggling week to week just to keep our heads above water. At one point we owed a vendor a couple of thousand dollars, and the rep came into the office to collect. I had to tell him that he'd have to wait a few more weeks, because we were spending what little money we had to attend the pool show.

He was not happy. He couldn't see past the dollar signs and realize that by attending that show we were investing in the company and committed to growth, which would mean a bigger account for him too if he could stick with us.

His reaction was a revelation for me. This guy's shortsightedness represented a mindset of lack and want, and I realized he didn't have what it would take to grow with us. We paid him off, but did very little business with him after that. Huge mistake on his part. Huge.

Not going to trade shows is the same kind of mistake in my opinion. In my years in the business I've found three specific reasons to keep attending trade shows, even when money is tight or business is crazy busy.

Reason One: The Products

We did end up going to that event, and I saw a huge array of new stuff. Amazing stuff, products my sales reps never showed me and things I never dreamed existed. The immersion in new products and technology was intense. It was a huge investment in my own knowledge base and worth the cost for that reason alone.

At another show several years ago, I came across a product that beautifully solved an ongoing problem we were having with our concrete slides. This was early on in the hybrid pool movement, and we didn't have a good solution for a finishing treatment.

We met a vendor using round penny tiles to surface a concrete slide. It was a wow moment for me, and I came home so excited. I took the crew back to six or seven previous jobs, stripped them down and used the penny tiles to resurface them. The customers were thrilled, and we were able to up our game and be ready for the next project.

Without speaking to this vendor face to face at the show, I never would have hit upon this particular solution. Industry shows give us the time to explore the off-book ideas or the "let's try this" moments that lead to real business breakthroughs.

Reason Two: The Relationships

In this industry, we walk that fine line between searching for the best price and getting the best perceived value. For me, it's important to build a supply chain I can rely on, so I can innovate and build with confidence.

Our Newly Tiled Slide

One vendor we'd worked with for years was Kafko Pool Products. We started using Kafko liners through a local supplier and loved the product. When our supplier closed we went direct to Kafko for our needs, building a good relationship with the folks in the manufacturing division.

When Latham came along and bought up the Kafko line, we were concerned that we'd be too small a fish for them to pay much attention to us. We needed this product; it was a crucial part of our supply chain.

By making a point to reach out to the Latham execs at industry events, we were able to get them invested and excited in what we were doing, and create a solid relationship with them, both on a business and a personal level. The supply chain remains intact, and we have a solid relationship at Latham.

Reason Three: The Hidden Solutions

Every once in a while you learn something at a show that completely changes the way you approach your work.

At one event I heard a presenter speaking about working with glass tile. He spoke about the science behind color theory, and my head started going a mile a minute. His ideas tapped into everything I had learned about art and design in school, and gave me an exact answer to all my questions about why color works the way it does. It has dramatically changed the way I approach color in my projects, and there's no way I would be this successful without that knowledge.

Sadly, I talk to a lot of pool guys in my local area who never go to the shows and see no reason to do so. And I hear those same folks grumbling that there's not enough business or too much competition in the industry.

To them I say "Get out there." Educate yourself, build relationships, and get inspired.

It not only helps your own business, it also raises the entire industry to the next level. Instead of being wary of our competition, let's work toward raising all of us up to the next level.

See you at the shows!

"Forget about keeping your customers happy. Keep yourself happy in your work, and that joy can't help but infuse everything you touch."

~ Al Curtis

16

WHY HAPPINESS MATTERS—TO YOU

By now it should be clear to you that happiness does indeed matter. Not only in how you feel at the end of the day, but in how your business grows and expands through the years.

I think back to the frigid spring day in the mud, whistling through the rain and the sleet. I think back to the vision of my end game, how excited and grateful I was to be engaged in this crazy, creative work. I can still feel that joy I felt that overcame the cold, the misery, the aches and pains.

I knew in that moment why happiness really matters.

How's Your Energy?

So now it's time for a gut check. What makes

you truly happy in your work? What are the moments when you simply lose yourself in the rhythm, the process, and find yourself humming along? Those are the moments that make a business, and indeed a life, worth doing.

In the next section, we'll help you get started on your own journey of discovering your "why," and translating that into action that can help you market your business and turn it into an epic adventure.

Part Four–What's Next for You?

"Build the right projects, at the right pace, for the right customers, with a high level of quality, creativity and design. Enjoy the work."

~ *Legendary Escapes Certain Way*

17

BACKFLIPS AND POOL FAIRIES— THE ART OF BRAND STORYTELLING

In the 1938 romantic comedy *Holiday*, Cary Grant's character Johnny Case has a signature way of dealing with the stresses of life. Whenever things get a little hairy, Case launches into a backflip to remind himself that life shouldn't be taken so seriously.

Eventually he finds true love after some vigorous gymnastics on New Year's Eve, and the final scene has him quite literally falling head over heels for Kathryn Hepburn's character.

It's brilliant storytelling, pure and simple, and the audience has no need for dialogue to understand exactly what's going on during his acrobatics. Grant's created a brand for himself in the course of the movie and we even come to expect his signature moves at key moments during the film.

Penny the Pool Dog in her Fairy Wings

Like Johnny Case, our Pool Guy Allan Curtis has been known to launch into a backflip or too. He's also strapped fairy wings onto his "Pool Dog" Penny, planted a pirate flag on a job site to stake his claim, and had a quick nap in a concrete tree at one pool. All of which have been shared on social media.

What's any of this have to do with selling pools?

For Legendary Escapes, it's got everything to do with this. It's the Pool Guy's story that sells pools, and it's that story that we use in our marketing efforts every day. With the range of technical tools out there for storytelling, we are able to create an almost unlimited amount of content that tells the story of Legendary Escapes and its founder Al.

Al Naps in the Tree

That backflip, for example, has become a phenomenal sales tool. The video of Al, perched atop one of his backyard creations, launching off the waterfall into the deep end only had around 80 views on YouTube; certainly not a viral success by social media standards. But from that video alone, we sold two six-figure pool projects in one season.

The reason is simple: the homeowners said they wanted to be able to do that in their own yards.

Engaging with storytelling is a long-standing practice of human culture. From the original clan around the fireplace in the evenings, the petroglyphs on ancient cave walls, the traveling bard of Shakespeare's time, to our current day obsession with movies and books, humans are wired for a good tale.

Brands have become keenly aware of this human connection, becoming masterful storytellers for their own companies.

Take Apple for instance. The launch of any new product instills not just excitement about the product itself, but an almost Pavlovian sense of envy. Is that because of the technology, or the story behind the product of belonging, early adoption and technical prowess that owning the latest Apple whatever bestows?

Or consider Dove's Campaign for Real Beauty, one of the first brands to embrace the healthy body image mantra by telling real people's stories about what it means to be beautiful, strong and healthy. The brand helped to launch a world-wide awareness of stereotypes and body-shaming rhetoric and turned on a whole generation of young women to a healthier approach to their bodies.

For both of these brands, it's not really about the products themselves, but the stories they tell that make them remarkable.

At Legendary Escapes, we take the same approach. If you look at our YouTube channel, very few of the videos are about the technical aspects of building a pool. You're more likely to see a clip of a happy customer and his kids barreling down the waterslide, Al, the ever present pool guy sharing some philosophy or thoughts on pool building, or Penny frolicking in the mud on a new build.

We started out on YouTube offering video clips answering frequently asked questions on in-ground pool care, and we still get a lot of traffic on those. Yet even in those technical clips, we always worked to instill great personality, a friendly attitude and a human connection through our Pool Guy persona.

According to marketing expert Deborah Shane[v], brand storytelling consists of a few key elements, including tapping into that element of real emotion.

"Include characters, personality, humor, pain and joy. Some of the best ways to accomplish this is through blogging, article writing, video, podcasting, webinars and workshops," she suggests.

Using real time examples of what you do is a good way to start, Shane notes. "Share specific examples of your brand in action including the product, process and people that make it happen."

In this way, your storytelling will be authentic and relatable, two keys to making all of this work for you. And don't be afraid to share your failures along with your successes, as this is all part of any brand's story.

Above all, be authentic. A friend of mine once worked for a company that pretended they were much bigger than they were. Customer service people (there were two of them) were asked to use several different names in their email replies to make it look like they had a huge team. The founder created a myth of himself as a "serial entrepreneur" to make him look like a tech heavy-hitter. And the marketing message was all geared about artificial limits on special offers (the "call within 10 minutes" mentality).

While the company offered a fantastic online service, it never thrived. The real story—of two really smart guys who created a brilliant solution eliminating a ton of drudgery for online marketers—got lost in the puffed-up story they told their audience, and themselves. They simply imploded under their own imaginary weight.

Find your own truth about what you do, and tell that story. Be real, be honest and be consistent with getting your content out there. If you do backflips, do backflips. If you serve your crew a barbeque lunch once a month, share those meals on YouTube. If you send a fruit basket at the end of the job, share pictures of your customer getting that special delivery on Instagram. Use the tools that are already there for you.

It's your story to tell. Tell it with pride.

18

LEVERAGING ORGANIC MARKETING AND YOUR SOCIAL SPHERE

Marketing as we know it has changed—dramatically. With the dawn of the social network, how we engage, interact and build our relationships has undergone a profound and irreversible shift. So how does a business owner or professional begin to play in the social sandbox?

You need a process to help you do just that; a simple to use and incredibly powerful tool for defining your marketing goals, creating an authentic and energetic online presence, and managing your interactions. We call it Organic Marketing.™ We start with a common tic-tac-toe concept, and use each square to flesh out your online signature, your connections, your social sphere, your customers, and six other critical elements that make up your overall marketing strategy. By methodically working on each square, you become comfortable in playing the game, making those "three across" connections and using social media as a powerful business tool.

There is no doubt about this: you need to be there. Show up with authenticity, with consistency, and with a clear understanding of how to connect the dots. When you put the right pieces in place to leverage your social sphere, your business will grow organically, and you will love the results!

Living in the Land of "What If..."

If social media is about stories and connecting people, it makes sense to start with a discussion of "what if."

If you enter the social media conversation asking how you can help, you're in the greatest power position you can imagine. When you care about what people are doing, you can be anywhere in the world, and people will pay attention to what you have to say. Stopping in to visit you online could be just the thing that they needed to feel good, get inspired, learn something, or create a new way of thinking.

Be open to the possibilities that new media opens up for you. Become part of a community that you want to grow with. You will become more like the people you associate with, so be sure to associate with good people. As Charlie

Tremendous Jones, in his book *Life is Tremendous* says, "You will be exactly who you are in five years with the exception of the people you associate with and the books that you read."[vi]

We invite you to read a book that could dramatically change your business, not just five years from now but beginning today. We wrote "Organic Marketing: A Guide to defining **Your Certain Way**" (2015) to help business owners understand their stories, and come from a place of authenticity when sharing those stories with the world.

It's the marketing process that we used to build Legendary Escapes into a successful, high-end boutique pool building company. And we've seen it help other business owners turn their dreams in realities, no matter what the field.

The beauty of Organic Marketing is that anyone can learn it; no marketing degree required.

You can find your copy on Amazon, then drop us an email at team@askthepoolguy.com and let us know you're diving in. We'll be your accountability partner and marketing idea bouncer on this journey.

We really look forward to meeting you, and sharing this part of your adventure!

With much enthusiasm and love,
Al & Sandi

Bonus Material

A Preview of Organic Marketing

THE RULES HAVE CHANGED

Organic Marketing in the Digital Age

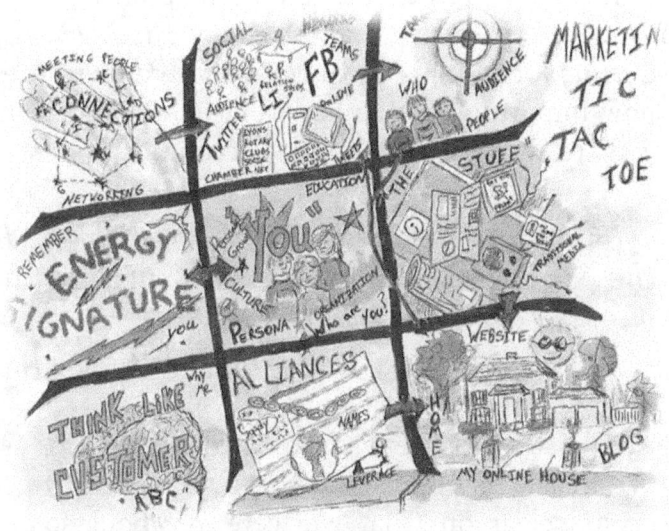

Organic Marketing Tic-Tac-Toe

You and I and most of the people reading this article are in the pool business. We know vinyl, tile and gunite. We understand pumps, filters and heaters. We are comfortable around excavators, cement mixers and pick-up trucks. We are hands-on, physical and results-focused.

It's no wonder, then, that so many of us would

rather do just about anything than try to decipher the foggy vagaries of marketing. Yet we're smart enough to know that, if we want our businesses to thrive, we somehow have to do just that.

Seeing Through the Fog

For Al and I, the fog started to lift about eight years ago as we began to study the philosophy of Wallace D. Wattles, and especially *The Science of Getting Rich.* In his writings, Wallace underscores how important it is to have a clear vision of who you are and what you hope to accomplish:

"The intensity of your desire will depend on the clearness of which you picture to yourself what you want to be."
~ *Wallace D. Wattles*

Those words were a watershed moment for us. We began to understand that we needed to get crystal clear on what we were all about so we could harness the energy required to make our business dreams a reality.

As we worked to define ourselves and our business in these terms, an amazing thing happened. An idea was born—so simple yet sublimely effective—that became the framework on which we built our entire marketing strategy.

The process, which we'll present to you over this and the following three articles, will help you begin to think in your certain way. This in turn will create social proof that the concepts are working, which will reinforce your belief. As you do, you will begin to notice dramatic shifts in your marketing, your business, and how you approach your work. We know we have.

And it's as easy as tic-tac-toe.

A New Marketing Paradigm

Marketing has changed dramatically over the past decade or so. How we engage, interact and build our relationships has undergone a profound and irreversible shift. So how does a business owner begin to thrive in the social sandbox?

What you need is a simple to use and powerful tool for defining your marketing goals, creating an authentic and energetic online presence, and managing your interactions. We call it Organic Marketing™.

What's required of you is that you commit to it. Show up with authenticity, with consistency, and with a goal of understanding how to connect the dots. When you put the right pieces in place to leverage your social sphere, your business will grow organically, and you will love the results!

"Everything that touches your life is an opportunity if you discover its proper use."
~ *Wallace D. Wattles*

The other thing that's required is a willingness to let go of your old notions of marketing, what works and what doesn't. We are living in a whole new digital world, and our customers are waiting for us in this playground. Let go and let this process unfold for you, and glean the insights along the way that will transform how you think and work.

The Marketing Bubble

To help understand what marketing really is for today's consumer, close your eyes and picture your ideal client. Next, picture a giant bubble around your client. This bubble isolates your client from anything that they haven't decided to pay attention to yet. We are exposed to more than 50,000 marketing messages each day; most just bounce off our bubbles. Your greatest challenge is to get your message inside of your ideal client's bubble.

Rather than piercing the bubble by force (popping), good marketing softens the edge of the bubble. By getting your message in front of your client as often as possible, perhaps by pulling up alongside the bubble unobtrusively, or being in the periphery, the person inside their bubble might begin to take notice. Hopefully they get closer to the edge of the bubble to peek outside.

Maybe you get them so curious that they will take their bubble even closer to your bubble.

(Think bumper bubbles; that's pretty cool!)

The more curious your prospect becomes, the more of your message you can share. Craft your message in a way that helps them identify their need for your service.

Once your prospect is paying attention, they are more likely to take action; it could be a purchase, a book mark for a later purchase, or sharing your message with people in their sphere of influence. In the world of social media, the goal is the share. You really, really want people to be sharing your messages with their own social networks.

A truly effective marketing campaign will have prospects in their bubbles vying for position trying to get a glimpse of what you have going on. Instead of selling anything to them, they are selling themselves on you, before you even have to start the sales process. Creating this kind of marketing becomes possible with our organic approach.

Some New Rules for an Old Game

Based on a tic-tac-toe board, with each of the nine squares representing a part of you and/or your business, the Organic Marketing process looks deceptively simple.

Beneath that simplicity, it's a powerful way to gain your prospects' attention and get them to allow you access to their bubble. The tic-tac-toe idea breaks down your marketing efforts into three categories—personal, business and universal—that when placed in a row in each axis of the board define the squares in relationship to each other.

The result is a visual short-hand to help you easily understand how to reach new audiences, build new relationships and grow your business.

What's Next?

We are often asked how social media is so different from traditional media. Here's the secret; it's not that different. Social media is not about using a new media in an old way. It's about using the new media to communicate with people in the way they choose. Understanding this makes all the difference in the world, and the tic-tac-toe concept will help you see it and put it into practice.

Join us online: AskThePoolGuy.com/Marketing

ABOUT THE AUTHORS

Allan Curtis, Sandi Maki

A founder who is part pool builder, part artist and part philosopher, with a dream of creating backyard experiences that are one-of-a-kind. A managing partner who isn't afraid to question everything to come up with a better way to work, play and live. A crew that is encouraged to pour nothing but good energy into everything they touch. Plus a healthy dose of think-outside-the-box marketing and inspirational thought leadership. That's the magic behind Legendary Escapes, a boutique hybrid pool building company in southeast Michigan.

Originally a vinyl pool building and service company, Al Curtis and Sandi Maki have grown Legendary Escapes into a sought-after premium pool building company by relentlessly striving to refine the work they do, who they do it for, and how they go about it. In the process, they have also created a business support group (aka the Insights Clubhouse) where small business owners gather to share innovative thinking on creating businesses and lives in which they can truly express their passions and their Certain Way.

Al and Sandi are both published authors, social media leaders and sought-after public speakers who are always willing to listen, learn, share and grow. Their enthusiasm is infectious, and their work speaks for itself.

Allan Curtis & Sandi Maki,
Ask the Pool Guy & Ask the Pool Girl

ADDITIONAL RESOURCES BY YOUR AUTHORS

To Enhance your Organic Marketing ™ Plans start here:

> Our Certain Way, The Building of a Legendary Pool Business (2015)
>
> Organic Marketing, A Guide to Defining Your Certain Way (2015)

Organic Marketing ™ Building Blocks and Follow Up:

> Social Media Explained* (2009)
> Social Media Strategies* (2010)
> Blogging Explained*(2009)
> Blogging Strategies*(2010)
> Organic Marketing ™ Explained* (2009)
> Organic Marketing ™ Advanced Strategies for Social Media* (2010)
> *Audio CD

Pool Resources:

> Ask the Pool Guy's Everyday Guide to Swimming Pools (2013)

Fun and Quirky Reads:

> 100 Marbles: How the Collective Mind, Gratitude and Masterminding Changed our Lives – A Journey through the InSights Mastermind (2013)

Heavy Breathing Just Before Midnight & Fuzzy New Socks (2013)

Developing your Certain Way:

The Science of Getting Rich by Wallace D. Wattles (2014)
The Science of Being Well by Wallace D. Wattles (2014)
The Science of Being Great by Wallace D. Wattles (2014)
The Science of Getting Rich by Wallace D. Wattles Audio – as read by Sandi Maki* (2011) *Audio CD

InSights Certain Way:

The Culture of InSights* (2010) *Audio CD

Industry Specific:
3 Dimensional Relationship Marketing for Dentists & the Psychology of Social Media* (2011) *Audio CD

www.askthepoolguy.com
www.insights-group.com

———————————

End notes

[i] Ware, Bronnie. (2012). *The Top Five Regrets of the Dying: A life Transformed by the Dearly Departing.* Carlsbad, CA: Hay House.

[ii] Sinek, Simon. (2011). *Start with Why: How Great Leaders Inspire Everyone to Take Action.* London: Portfolio Publishing.

[iii] Kahn, Peggy. (1984). *the Handy Girls Can Fix It!* Random House for Young Readers.

[iv] IbisWorld Market Research on Swimming Pool Construction in the U.S., 2013.

[v] Shane, Debra. "What is Brand Storytelling?" *Small Biz Trends*. 28 May 2015. Web. 15 Sept. 2015.

[vi] Jones, Charlie. (1981). *Life Is Tremendous*. Tyndale Momentum Press.